D1520380

YANKEE
DOODLE

Cavendish
Square

New York

JENNIFER REED

Published in 2020 by Cavendish Square Publishing, LLC
243 5th Avenue, Suite 136, New York, NY 10016

Copyright © 2020 by Cavendish Square Publishing, LLC

First Edition

Website: cavendishsq.com

This publication represents the opinions and views of the author based on his or her personal
experience, knowledge, and research. The information in this book serves as a general
guide only. The author and publisher have used their best efforts in preparing this book and
disclaim liability rising directly or indirectly from the use and application of this book.

All websites were available and accurate when this book was sent to press.

Library of Congress Cataloging-in-Publication Data

Names: Reed, Jennifer, 1967- author.
Title: Yankee Doodle / Jennifer Reed.
Description: New York, NY : Cavendish Square Publishing, 2020. | Series: America's songs |
Audience: Grades 2-5 | Includes bibliographical references and index.
Identifiers: LCCN 2019000918 (print) | LCCN 2019001081 (ebook) | ISBN 9781502648808 (ebook) |
ISBN 9781502648792 (library bound) | ISBN 9781502648778 (pbk.) | ISBN 9781502648785 (6 pack)
Subjects: LCSH: Yankee Doodle (Song)--Juvenile literature.
Classification: LCC ML3561.Y2 (ebook) | LCC ML3561.Y2 R43 2020 (print) | DDC 782.42/15990973--dc23
LC record available at https://lccn.loc.gov/2019000918

Editorial Director: David McNamara
Editor: Kristen Susienka
Copy Editor: Nathan Heidelberger
Associate Art Director: Alan Sliwinski
Designer: Joe Parenteau
Production Coordinator: Karol Szymczuk
Photo Research: J8 Media

Printed in the United States of America

CONTENTS

The Old Guard Fife and Drum Corps plays patriotic tunes during a Presidents' Day celebration at Mount Vernon in 2014.

CHAPTER 1

A Silly Song

The United States has many songs about it and the people living in it. Some of these songs talk about how beautiful the United States is. Other songs talk about silly things in America. Some silly songs are important to Americans today. One example is "Yankee Doodle." It started as a song making fun of Americans. Today, it is a **patriotic** song.

Yankee Doodle

Yan - kee Doo - dle   went to town   ri - ding on a   po - ny,

Stuck a feath - er   in his cap and   called it mac - a - ro - ni.

Yank - ee Doo - dle,   keep it up,   Yan - kee Doo - dle   dan - dy,

Mind   the mu - sic   and   the step, and   with the girls be   han - dy.

Making It Their Own

"Yankee Doodle" was a popular British song in the late 1700s. Its **melody** was played at dances during this time. Words for the song were written in the mid-1700s. No one knows who wrote the original words. The song had different versions. The most well-known version was not a very nice song. It made fun of Americans. That is because America and Britain were at war. The war was the American Revolution. It happened from 1775 to 1783.

The British called Americans "yankees." A "doodle" was a silly person. A "yankee doodle" was a silly American.

During the war, Americans started to sing the song at battles. They liked to make fun of themselves. The song's happy melody

♪ **FACT**

The word "doodle" comes from the German word *dudel*. It means "fool."

This image shows American colonists on the streets of New York City on Christmas Day in the 1700s.

made Americans feel good. Soon, the song united the American soldiers. It helped them win America's freedom from Britain.

Singing It Today

Today, the song is a silly song for kids to sing. People also sing it or hear it played at celebrations and parades. The Fourth of July is a good time to hear the song. It is a song that Americans can enjoy whenever they hear it.

FACT

England was the world's most powerful country during the American Revolution. It ruled countries on almost every continent.

What Does It Mean?

Originally, British soldiers sang "Yankee Doodle." It poked fun at the Americans they were fighting. Its meaning has changed now. However, the song's **message** is still silly. The words in the song lots of people know today talk about a man riding on a pony and trying to become someone he isn't. Many words in the song had different meanings in the eighteenth century than they have today. If you understand the old-fashioned words, you can understand the song better.

Words to Know

dandy A person who thinks he looks good in the way he dresses.
doodle A fool.
handy Within easy reach to help.
macaroni A fashionable person.
Yankee A negative word the British used to call American colonists.

This illustration shows silly Yankee Doodle riding his horse and wearing a feather in his hat. People cheer him in the background.

Here, American colonists "mind their step," or dance, in the early 1700s.

CHAPTER 2

Yankee Doodle, Keep It Up!

In the 1700s, America was ruled by England. People who lived in America during that time were called colonists. America was a colony. A colony is a country that belongs to another country.

The melody of "Yankee Doodle" was first heard in the 1700s. People liked the melody. They began to

play it at dances. People invented steps to the dance. That might be one reason why the song talks about minding the step, or remembering the dance moves.

A Doctor and a Songwriter

From 1754 to 1763, the British and French fought a war in North America. It was called the French and Indian War. It was during this war that the first words were

FACT

In 1775, the United States was producing much of the world's iron.

put to "Yankee Doodle." The man who wrote these words is thought to be Dr. Richard Shuckburgh. He was a doctor in the British army. Shuckburgh wrote several verses. The war ended in 1763.

Soon after, American colonists began to be upset by British laws. They wanted to become their own country. New battles started in 1775. The American

This painting by Edwin Willard Deming shows Native American soldiers surprising British soldiers in an attack during the French and Indian War.

Revolution began. In 1776, American colonists signed the Declaration of Independence. This document said that America was its own country. The war got worse after people signed the declaration. The war lasted until 1783.

During the American Revolution, new words to "Yankee Doodle" were written. They made fun of the Americans George Washington and John Hancock.

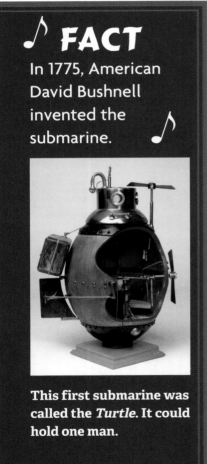

♪ **FACT**

In 1775, American David Bushnell invented the submarine. ♪

This first submarine was called the *Turtle*. It could hold one man.

A Song for the Troops

"Yankee Doodle" became a song the British sang a lot. Army bands played it during battles. The British even sang it on the first day of the war. Then, the British began losing the war. The Americans watched the British leave the battlefield. As they left, Americans sang "Yankee Doodle." It became a song of America after that. More Americans started to play and sing it.

This illustration shows American colonists getting angry with the British soldiers marching in the streets.

Americans took the song "Yankee Doodle" and made it their own. They added funny words that helped the American soldiers' **morale** during the war. Some of their words made fun of Britain's King George III and British soldiers. Other words

King George III was ruler of Great Britain during the American Revolution.

celebrated American leaders, like George Washington. New words were often added during the war. A British soldier wrote, "It was not a little mortifying to hear them play this tune."

Other Examples

Soon, other people wrote different words to the song. A man named Edward Bangs wrote new words in 1775 or 1776. His song was called "A Farmer and His Son's Return from a Visit to the Camp." Later, it got a new name, called "Boston Yankee Doodle Ballad." Bangs was both a college student at Harvard University and a type of soldier called a **minuteman**. Minutemen could get ready for

The words to Edward Bangs's song "A Farmer and His Son's Return" appear here, under a drawing of people playing music.

battle very quickly. They helped the American army during the American Revolution.

"A Farmer and His Son's Return" was printed on a sheet of paper called a broadside. It was published in

1775 or 1776. It had fifteen verses! This is the earliest recorded printing of a version of "Yankee Doodle."

The version of the song that many people sing today was published in 1842. It was part of a book called *The Nursery Rhymes of England* by James Orchard Halliwell.

This is a sketch of James Orchard Halliwell.

Timeline

- **1754–1763** The French and Indian War is fought.

- **1755** Dr. Richard Shuckburgh writes the first known version of "Yankee Doodle."

- **1775–1776** Edward Bangs, a Harvard student and minuteman, writes fifteen new verses to "Yankee Doodle." The new lyrics poke fun at the colonists, but more so at the British.

- **1775** The American Revolution begins, and the submarine is invented.

- **1776** The Declaration of Independence is signed.

- **1783** The American Revolution ends with the signing of the Treaty of Paris.

- **1800s–Present** "Yankee Doodle" becomes a classic patriotic song.

Young children sing during a Fourth of July parade.

CHAPTER 3

A Celebrated Song

Today, most people learn "Yankee Doodle" when they are young. It is a popular children's nursery **rhyme**. The nursery rhyme is fun to sing and dance to. However, people sing the song at other times too. Many people play or sing the song around the Fourth of July. The song has also appeared in TV shows and movies.

Yankee Doodle Disney

In 1980, Walt Disney Productions released a patriotic **record**. It had popular Disney characters Mickey Mouse, Donald Duck, and Goofy singing patriotic songs. The

Disney's *Yankee Doodle Mickey* features many patriotic songs, including "Yankee Doodle."

name of the record was *Yankee Doodle Mickey*. "Yankee Doodle" was one of the songs on the record.

FACT
"Yankee Doodle" is the US state of Connecticut's official state song.

Tom and Jerry

Starting in the 1940s, Tom and Jerry were famous cartoon

characters. Tom was a cat and Jerry was a mouse. Tom always tried to catch Jerry. He wanted to eat him. In 1943, during World War II, a cartoon of Tom and Jerry was made. It was called *The Yankee Doodle Mouse*. In the movie, Tom tries to catch Jerry. Jerry is smarter than Tom, though. In the end, a rocket explodes and forms the American flag. Jerry **salutes** the flag. This short film encouraged

FACT
The town of Billerica, Massachusetts, was named "America's Yankee Doodle Town" on July 25, 1999.

the troops to keep fighting during World War II, just like "Yankee Doodle" encouraged soldiers in the American Revolution.

Tom and Jerry were in many cartoons. Tom would always chase Jerry, but he could never catch him.

Presidential Pet

"Yankee Doodle" even inspired the name of Caroline Kennedy's pet. Caroline Kennedy was the daughter of President John F. Kennedy. She got a pony in 1962. She named him Macaroni. He got his name from the song

Caroline Kennedy rides Macaroni in a 4-H Club horse show in 1964.

"Yankee Doodle." Macaroni became a very popular pet. He even got mail! He was on the cover of *Life* magazine with Caroline in September 1962. He got special gifts

from people around the world. Sometimes Caroline rode Macaroni at the White House.

No matter how old you are, you can enjoy "Yankee Doodle" for its silly words. But also remember that it wasn't so silly at first. Still, it is now a popular song many Americans can enjoy.

The Song Today

Some famous people and characters have sung the song. For example, on the TV show *Sesame Street*, Kermit the Frog helped songwriter puppet Don Music write new words. The new words talk about making a dish of macaroni. The characters didn't realize "macaroni" had a different meaning in the 1700s!

Kermit the Frog sings during a show.

GLOSSARY

melody The main part in a piece of music that people sing.

message The main meaning of a piece or work, like a song.

minuteman A type of soldier from the American Revolution that could get ready for battle quickly.

morale Having a positive attitude about something; confidence or enthusiasm.

patriotic Relating to love of a country.

record A disk with grooves that has sound, usually music, and is played by using a phonograph or record player.

rhyme Words that sound the same at the end of a line in poetry.

salute To raise your right hand to your forehead, showing respect to something.

FIND OUT MORE

Books

Mara, Wil. *If You Were a Kid During the American Revolution*. New York: Scholastic Library Publishing, 2017.

Thompson, Ben. *Guts & Glory: The American Revolution*. Boston, MA: Little, Brown Books for Young Readers, 2017.

Websites

DK Find Out!: American Revolution

https://www.dkfindout.com/us/history/american-revolution

DK Find Out is an educational site with a specific page on the American Revolution. It includes biographies, information about battles and important documents, and more.

Kids Environment Kids Health: Yankee Doodle

https://kids.niehs.nih.gov/games/songs/patriotic/yankee-doodle/index.htm

This page from the National Institute of Environmental Health Sciences features the song "Yankee Doodle."

Video

Sesame Street: Don Music Writes "Yankee Doodle"

https://www.youtube.com/watch?v=-M30g3In8ao

Watch Don Music, Kermit the Frog, and friends write new words to "Yankee Doodle."

INDEX

ABOUT THE AUTHOR

Jennifer Reed has written over forty books for children and teens. She is married to a former Naval fighter pilot and has a love for the United States military and the history of the United States. Some of her books have been about the US military. She lives in Vermont and has a direct view of historical places Lake Champlain and Fort Ticonderoga, where she continues to gather inspiration and ideas.